# A
# STRUGGLE
# EQUALS
# GOALS

# A
# STRUGGLE
# EQUALS
# GOALS

*Macena L. Mason*

ARPress
ILLUMINATING IDEAS, EMPOWERING VOICES

**ARPress**
45 Dan Road Suite 5
Canton MA 02021
Hotline:            1(888) 821-0229
Fax:                1(508) 545-7580

Ordering Information:

Quantity sales. Special discounts are available on quantity purchases by corporations, associations, and others. For details, contact the publisher at the address above.

Printed in the United States of America.

ISBN-13:            Softcover        979-8-89356-420-4

                    eBook            979-8-89356-419-8

Library of Congress Control Number: 2024904628

# Table Of Contents

I would like to think everyone who played a part in my life.
You gave me the strength to set my goals.

# Acknowledgments

For me, this one section is very hard to write because there are special people in my family who have done something special for me. Some things are very common and other things are not so common. Some of them do not know how special they are too me.

I thank my mother for being my support. My mother acted as my mother and father and allowed me to grow. Learning to grow was and still is very important to me. I am grateful for the skill that I have learned and the time spent by my grandmother who was there to help my mother out.

To my mother and father's families, I hope you are able to see all that was lost by not being near me. In return, you have made me push the door open that you have kept the locks on for so long to see the outside world, even after I have been damaged. I also thank my friends that I met at Prince George's Community College because they do not know that I also call them "My Family" as well. My friends have started to fill a big gap in my heart.

I also thank other family members for being part of my support system and making me feel good. I now thank my father for a new father and daughter relationship in the future. I also thank Mr. Pettis for his knowledge in publishing and for helping me to publish this, my first, autobiography.

I also thank anyone else who also worked on this autobiography. You have my sincere thanks in all that you have done with your time, effort, and skills. I also would like to thank my aunt Renee Young for her knowledge of the computer system and for the time she spent in making the last changes to this book. She is a very special aunt.

Lastly, I thank God for all that He has done for me in the first 25 years of my life. I thank God for all that He has give me. I also thank Him for protecting me while He allows me to achieve all of my goals.

Thank You, God!

The names to people in my life and places were changed to protect those that I love.

# CHAPTER 1

## RAISING ME & COMING INTO THE WORLD

I first came into the world on May 2, 1973. May 2nd also happened to be my mother's birthday before it became mine. So, it is a really special day for me because I get to share it with a really special mother.

Six months after I was born, I had a febrile seizure and my kidney on my left side did not form properly. The two conditions do not go together, and I didn't know that it would change me from having or knowing about a normal life.

As time went by, I grew up into what felt like a glorious world. Everything around me felt perfect. The people around me felt perfect. These people, at my young age, were my family, but I didn't know that at the time. So, because this was all that I really saw all the time, I thought everyone looked or acted like them for at least the first five to six years of my life. The answer to that thought turned out to be something else when it was time for me to go to school for the first time and deal with the outside world on my own. It came out to be that nobody was perfect.

My grandmother and my mother would give me medicine everyday. Believe it or not, when I was little, I didn't understand what it was that I was taking this medication for. I also knew that I went to the doctors every so often as well. I didn't understand how different it would make me from the other children I would deal with once I was in school. Nobody could tell me what it was within me that made it impossible for me to make friends.

I couldn't figure out for myself why anyone would not want to be friends with someone that was nice. I didn't know what was making me look, feel, act, be, or even do things differently from them.

What people don't understand is that the medication that epileptics take changes their physical, emotional, and mental appearance. It makes us a totally different person on the inside and outside. We can look like you on the inside and outside, but we may also not be physically, emotionally, or mentally as well as you. This is due to the control the medication has over us. Some people cannot understand this until they either live the life themselves or get information and take the time to read it.

My grandmother was a large part of my life and I loved her like my second mother. However, she was very tight on me very protective. I had to do my best to break away from her, although she acted like my true mother. It wasn't my real mother that I needed to break away from. My real mother was always ready for me to mature. My grandmother was never ready, no matter how much older she herself had become. This only served to increase her hold on me. All of this made it very difficult to break free to mature and become my own person. Often, my epileptic condition made me want to be more independent and like everyone else.

The only good things that I can say about being close to my grandmother are the things that I learned that have made me both mentally and emotionally smart today. Through my grandmother, I learned a lot of my cooking, sewing, and skills with antiques. Though her tightness also came with a lot of love, there were other things that she could not give to me that I had to get on my own like other people do. The world does not give you everything. Some things you have to feed to yourself.

I can admit that because of our closeness, every now and then, pain can still linger in me. Especially when you get used to socializing in one particular atmosphere. Once you visit another you feel emotionally different. Personally, I feel like I have played a hopping game like a kangaroo with emotions to please everyone.

When school started, for me that was like being "born" for the second time. This is because I had never been around a lot of people who looked like or talked liked me. Pre-school came and went. I started grade school, which I will call St. John, a catholic school. There, my emotional life changed for the rest of my life. Where I was this happy little girl, I was now a sad little girl as I had said before, nobody would play with me. I was a different person. I did not know or understand why I was different, but this confusion and pain went on every day for the rest of my school life.

Every day, I would try to find a way to make friends. When we would have gym class, I was the one picked last. Nobody wanted me on their team because I was not fast enough. However, they had no choice. I was in the gym class too. I had to go somewhere because I had to play too. I had to get a grade just as the others did. That I was chosen because I had to be was devastating. Would you like this to happen to you too?

People didn't realize it, but I was crying on the inside. I would cry even louder when I was on the school parking lot where we would have recess and again when I would get home. Every night I would pray to God for a best friend, hoping that my prayer would come true. It did, but not until the second grade. This friendship lasted for a good while.

My anger and pain would build because I was not as strong as most people. I could not take the mental abuse. Over the years, I felt emotionally down. It took a long time for me to feel mentally mature. When I was little, I cried every minute of the day. Today, I try to write out my emotions and be more mature about it if it is possible.

People hurt me often when I was small because they knew that it was easy and fun for them. The way it looks over the years, it was as if they had nothing better to do. Emotionally and physically, I did not know how to stop the abuse or the pain no matter what adults like my father would tell me. I grew up with adults telling me how to feel hurt even though I had never felt that emotion before in my whole life. The only emotional feeling that I had grown up with was happiness since I had been protected from the outside world.

All of this was wrong. I would never have had to experience the pain from the outside world that I did if I had grown up experiencing it little by little as a child. I could have learned about the pain before it hurt me then I would have been able to recognize it. School would have been a lot more fun. I could have handled the children better if I had had a better understanding of myself. Physical activities that I could not do would not have seemed like a big mental or physical problem to me. I would have had the answers needed for myself and for those who wanted to bother me for what they didn't understand. I could have been an even stronger person.

I noticed that I was not going to get a lot of friends like the other children had. So, it made me want to "run away." This running away did not mean that I would not come back. I just wanted to do something to get away from those people that would not become close to me. So I started doing things in school during recess time to make me feel good about myself and so I could have the same amount of fun as everyone else. I started looking for a small activity I could do at school. The activity did not matter to me. I just wanted to get away from my pain. So, at St. John, I became a Safety Patrol Guard. A Safety Patrol Guard is someone who protects and makes sure that others are okay.

On my lunch breaks, I would go on the first through third grade recess lot and help the teacher in making sure that the children on the lot were okay. Doing this everyday while in school kept me busy and made me happy again. The children loved me and it made me feel good about myself. I had also gotten an award for doing this job. Doing this help me to set more little goals for myself.

I did another activity in school as well, Girl Scouts. Physically, the activity was fun for what you get to do to earn the badges and for going on the camping trips. On a personal note, for me it wasn't as exciting as it was for everyone else because I still didn't get to make any friends in the group, which is why I had joined the club in the first place. So, in reality, I didn't meet my goal when joining the Girl Scout Troop. I didn't get out of the Girl Scout Troop what they said girls got who joined the group.

Later on, when I saw that making friends wasn't working in school as well as I had hoped it would. I started pushing myself more on the mental side of my life. When I saw other people getting things that I wanted I couldn't figure out how in the world to get those same things. These same people already had the friends, and now they were getting awards, too. That wasn't fair! I said to myself. I wanted some of that.

You could not go up to the teacher and just ask for the awards. So, I started praying and believing that my name would be called. I worked hard in making myself noticeable to the teacher. I listened and asked for any extra work that could be done to raise my grade. Especially when I was having trouble. I always checked to make sure that it was correct.

I received my first academic awards in Religion and Special Effort. These awards have made me so proud over the years. Since then, I have not stopped working hard. I have gained other awards over the years as well. A list of the awards are in Chapter 7 of this book. Some of my awards over the years, I have gotten more than once. My awards and goals together equal my age up to this point, which is twenty-five.

# CHAPTER 2

## TIME TO LEARN

A family can make living bad for a child with epileptic seizures. My parents and family, even though it was all out of love, made the biggest mistake that they could have made: I was an overprotected child. I did not realize it. I thought that I was learning everything that I needed to know, but I was not. The protection is like living with your eyes closed. The only things that could come in were what my family wanted me to see, not what I needed to see.

By the time I started school, I was like a baby in a young child's body. Another child would be considered worldly because of all of the things that it could mentally, emotionally, or physically understand very quickly—street lingo, sex, relationships, handling oneself on the street, gangs, and possibly bad words. I was considered to be an unworldly child because I was much slower to understand these things. I would not have gotten this information overnight. Patience would have been necessary for me to learn any of it. Once people have the impression that you cannot learn the same information as them, they never seem to see what you can accomplish.

A big mistake of my mother and grandmother's was in allowing me to grow up isolated. I couldn't learn about the outside world from my family. I could not have conversations with people not visible to me. I did not succeed conversationally because most people did not want to talk with me.

Over a lot of time, this has gotten a little better, but there are things still a lot of gaps in this skill. Mentally and emotionally, it can be difficult practicing this skill with a disorder like epilepsy because every time I would become sick, I would lose a lot of information in my short-term memory. Many times, I would not know what it was that I had lost until I had a need for the information.

Just as a child can be dependent on a parent for everything, I had become dependent on calendars, notepads, pen, and pencils as my second memory where my short-term memory has let me down. I forget names of relatives, friends, and locations. My forgetfulness is not out of cruelty or rudeness to others it is a side effect of having epilepsy, which is physically hard to control.

I do not know what I did that was so wrong, but my own family acted as if they didn't trust me. This is how I picture myself. They could trust other people with information about themselves, but could not trust me. Growing up around them, my family, at times, tended to act ashamed about themselves. If I as a child found out about one of their secrets, they would go into an emotional fit. My family did not see me as a person growing up as they did. But I still had to grow up, even with my disorder. I still had to learn the same living skills that they knew.

Today, because of my inner lifestyle, there are things I still do not understand. For example, I don't understand street terms or slang and there are things that are out on the street that still can be confusing. I am not trying to say that because I want to know this information, I want to live this type of lifestyle. I want to mentally understand as much as possible, so there is no emotional confusion. However, what little I know now, I had to learn on my own.

Growing up, not being able to do the same things as others or those around me (who were adults) can be difficult. I could be made to feel bad about something simple. An example is a conversation with my friend on the telephone. All I wanted (and still do), was to be able to have the same pleasure as those around me. One was talking on the telephone. There was a day when my grandmother made me get off the phone for no apparent reason. Whenever, I would see her on the telephone, I would see how happy it would make her feel by the expression on her face. All I wanted was the same enjoyment as my grandmother on the telephone as her. I would see how happy it would make her feel by the expression on her face. I feel that everyone should have the right and chance to be able to be happy with other people.

Parents and relatives have to remember not to over protect and have conversations with their child about everything that is in the outside world. These include things like sex, relationships, and emotions.

A special time that is so clear to me, was when I was 13 years old. My mother timed it just right. She brought home this pamphlet that explained my menstrual cycle. She read it with me and explained it to me. Like clockwork, the very next day, I had my menstrual cycle. What made it special was that my mother did not make me ashamed of myself for something that is very natural. To this day, I see it as part of my life.

I was 16 years old when another conversation took place with my mother. I consider this to be another special time or moment. Because I grew up in what seemed like a quiet and sheltered world, I thought I knew what the answer was already. I felt that if I couldn't have the understanding of everything in the outer world, then that meant that I couldn't deal with other people as well. The conversation I had with my mother was about boys. If I was an overprotected child, then that meant I couldn't speak to them. I was wrong about my answer. She had even asked me my opinion, which was unexpected. She surprised me with her feelings. She also gave me support. She even told me to go outside more during the spring and summer to meet them. So, a person with this disorder or any disorder for that matter, does not have to be closed in or overprotected all of their life.

## Father's Side

Life on my father's side was (and still is) not much better than that of my mother's side. I could participate in the inside world activities, but I was still separated from the outside world. Examples are cooking, cleaning, decorating, or writing. It's another thing to be somewhere where I could not participate at all and still cannot. My family on my father's side never allowed me to get near them. I have always felt sheltered from really knowing who they were. It hurt to be kept from the chance of knowing my family completely. Every now and then, I might get lucky and have a good experience with my family.

It has been hard growing up with epilepsy and having a father and family that seemed as if they did not want to understand you at all. To start with, my father made it difficult for me. Instead of trying to be proud of me for being responsible for my life, he chose to go in the opposite direction.

The age of 16 is when teenagers are happy because this is the time when they can get a learner's permit to drive. At this time, I really wanted to drive. Then I found out that people like me had to be seizure free for three months in order to get a permit. The information upset me because I had been looking forward to driving. Since I was not seizure free, I chose not to get my permit.

My father asked me about learning to drive one day while in the car with him to go to an event. I had thought that when I told him my decision, he would have backed me up for making the right decision. I was wrong. He was not able to emotionally understand my decision. He was against it. He would have rather had me make the wrong decision, which would have been lying to get my learner's permit. I knew that I would not have been able to live with myself. I would have been lying to myself. I also would have feared hurting someone if an accident had occurred. I knew that I could not control anything that happens when I am sick. So, the only logical and best thing for me to do was to not get my learner's permit at all. It has been better this way because I also get to learn more about my independence when I am both mentally and physically out on my own.

Over the years, I have also grown up to where I really wanted to be a part of the same activities that I enjoyed with my mother's side of the family. When I would see my father's side, I was never allowed to bring items or make food for the picnics. Just coming made me feel out of place. I would see others in my family and even their friends being allowed to do it, but I couldn't. I felt as if I was not good enough. As time passed, I grew more and more hurt. One of my family members went so far as to use my disorder, not my name, to introduce me to one of her friends or relatives that I had never met. I am looked at as a child by my adult relatives I am not allowed to participate as others (in a giving way), but my life is allowed to be spread about and looked at in their own way. My father's family has never taken the time to talk to me or to learn and understand about my condition. Trips over the years have become difficult with my family, especially my father. My father doesn't understand how the medicine I take can affect my body, making it difficult to do a lot of physical activity without taking rest breaks. Because of my quick exhaustion, I have to take more rest breaks than the normal persons to keep from becoming sick. It has become disappointing that I cannot do a lot of things with my father to keep from having the arguments and the bad feelings about this disorder and myself. It's hard to look at myself sometimes and see one image and mentally know that I am something else on the inside. I can look fine on the outside, but feel really drained and tired on the inside.

Family engagements, whether on my mother or father's side of the family, have never been the greatest. It has always been very lonely for me. I never knew how to speak to any of them and when I would try, I would not get any response back. Seeing relatives conversing with other relatives is very hard. I felt left out because I did not grow up with anyone, like a brother, sister, or even cousins around me though my mother and father did. Growing up with relatives your own age would make you a stronger person. Growing up alone tends to make you feel emotionally weak inside because every time I would see these people, I was alone, just as I was in school.

So, I grew to feel envious of what I saw. It pushed me to want to make my own personal family of friends to fill the big gap that had been left in my heart. You can make your new family big or small to fill the gap. I started out a very sensitive, closed, and hidden person while maturing. You may also still have a small hole in your mind and heart for your family. There are times when I still do.

# CHAPTER 3

## LEARNING ON MY OWN: SETTING GOALS

When I was 13 years old, I started noticing that other children could do things that I couldn't. These were things that I thought only adults did or that adults taught you when your age came. Like you learn how to walk by the time you are at least two, not ten years old! Well, I started noticing that there were children out in the world, children my age, who were already doing a lot of adult things. It was bad enough that as a child I couldn't fight for myself. No, I wasn't a strong child growing up. So, when I saw that these same children, especially the ones who gave me trouble in school everyday, could do these things, then I wanted to do them, too.

What really pushed my nerve button or made me mad was that these kids looked like me. These kids were black kids also. These black kids were probably from Washington, DC coming over into my area, Lanham, MD. It made me angry inside to see this.

The only thing I needed though was the support at home to do what I wanted to do, which was to learn how to ride the Metro bus to start. I had asked my mother about it and she was supportive about me learning and wanting to do it. When my grandmother found out, she was upset with me. I was surprised to see her anger. I thought that she would have been just as supportive as my mother for wanting to see me grow up. That wasn't the case at all. She was just plain scared for me.

I was determined to do this, though. I knew inside that there were children my age who could do it whether or not they lived in the area.

I became what I call "sneaky girl" from them on. I stopped telling my grandmother everything because I saw that everything that I might like, she might not like. It had also set me up for more goals after I saw that I had accomplished my first one, which was riding the Metro bus. I have been doing it ever since. Now it has been 12 years.

My grandmother and others can go and do a lot of the things that they want to do on their own. I personally don't have to be dependent on anyone if I don't want to or have to, for a lot of little trips. I can go places on my own and be back when I want to, on my own free time.

Because of my personal life and goals, I have cut back on doing a lot of the close things I did when I was a little girl with my grandmother. This doesn't mean that I don't like these things. This just mean that my interests for myself have changed over time and because of my personal health, I have to take care of myself differently. A lot of things that other people like, I personally can't take for long periods of time. So, to keep myself happy, I have to get out of them quickly because usually most people aren't going to do the things that I need or I may need something too many times. So, to stay mentally, emotionally, and sometimes physically happy, I just have to get out of what other people like when they start to affect me in a negative way.

Another goal that I set was that I was going to try to stand up to people more. I was getting tired of people looking down on me because of my illness. I am not saying that I was able to stop them from doing it, but I had to start getting rid of some of the pain. In my early years, I did this with my grandmother. Yes!! The same one that I told you loved me. I stood up to her to break the cycle for the first time. Breaking the cycle for me was to get her to see that I was growing up to be a young lady, like she was an older lady. One day, she was going to have to leave me alone and let me do things for myself and allow me to make my own choices and decisions. Choices like riding the Metro bus.

One day, I got my nerves together and stood up to her. For me, this was very difficult, especially when you have always loved someone all of your life and someone, to you, looks physically bigger than you. Maybe their voice has always sounded stronger than yours. So, while she was sitting down, I took my time and let out my feelings. I told her how I had felt and that she had to start letting me go to grow up to do the things that I wanted to do so that I could learn on my own like everyone else. Emotionally, all of this was difficult. For the first time, I was standing over my grandmother and it felt weird.

She didn't want to let go, and it has taken a lot of time. Whether she agreed to it or not, I still went ahead with what I wanted to do, which was to grow up.

Afterwards, I found that other people may have looked at and seen me differently from a lack of understanding my goals, accomplishments, and illness. From an aunt, I found out that my cousins in my family didn't like me because of what I had done or was able to do. It wasn't my fault. I couldn't help that I was an only child. I also couldn't help the time that I was born or the person to whom I was born.

The condition that I have helped me to make better choices because it had already pulled my life down from the very beginning. I didn't want to be pulled down anymore than what I was, so I tried my best to love everyone. Yet, everyone couldn't see and love me in the same way that I had loved them. I fight with this feeling every time I see my family. Which is why I say that there are only a few people in my family that I have been allowed speak to. One is my uncle on my mother's side.

When my mother chose him also to be my godfather, I believe she made a very good decision. Believe it or not, he actually gets mad if he doesn't hear from me in a long time. My problem was that I was too scared to call. I would always guess that he would be too busy to speak because most people that I have ever tried to speak to never had the time to speak to me.

The other person is my other uncle on my father's side. He is also emotionally nice as well. I can speak to him about our family as well. He was the only one, when I was little, who acted as if he were my friend, and not just my uncle. Over time, my trust in him built up as well.

I have spent time over the years doing different activities. I would do these different things to help teach myself and help myself with my social skills. Growing up, I was a shy child. A shy child meant that I was a very quiet child. This made socializing in school, family, and other outside places difficult. It was bad enough that I spoke with a slow mind, and still do. It doesn't mean that I am stupid, just slower. It takes me longer to verbalize my thoughts. Because there were social things that I didn't know how to do as well, I took my summer, starting at the age of 14, and used it to practice my social skills.

Since I had no friends to socialize with on a daily basis, I would go to the pool everyday during the summer and practice speaking to people there. This was one of my social skills goals that I couldn't work on very well at school. So, I worked on it during the summer at the pool.

Another goal that I had, which I also worked on at the pool, was my swimming. Believe it or not, I was afraid of the water. My mother would put me into summer camp when I was little and they would try to teach me how to swim by holding me in the water. I was afraid of swimming because I thought that these people would drop me. I didn't know them well enough to trust them to hold me in the water. So at 14, I took the time to read in the encyclopedia about swimming and learned how to swim.

When I went to the pool everyday, I would practice swimming to the wall of the pool to make me feel safe. I would do whatever the encyclopedia told me to. I then took up swimming lessons to build up my skill some more, after my confidence was built up enough. Now, I can swim to at least five feet of water. I can float and swim on my back a little. The most I have to learn now is the treading part for the eight feet or deeper water. Nonetheless, I can get in the water and still have fun like other people.

When I was 15 and 16 years old, I worked on other social skills as well. These social skills also helped me to speak to people, and helped me to learn about myself and what I could do for other people. By this time during the summer, I began volunteer work.

The first two places that I volunteered at were in hospitals. This, for me, felt like a real job even though I didn't get paid. I enjoyed them a lot. I always hated the fact that I had to leave to go back to school. Since then, I have volunteered in other places, such as the American Red Cross. Doing these things teaches me how to work with others and the best things about myself as a person. For example, I know that kids love me. I am also more patient with kids than some other adults might be.

Throughout my life, I have spent time doing other activities as well. Some of these activities I did for only a short period of time, while others I did on and off. Some were playing games like T-ball when I was about seven years old, and taking ballet lessons between the ages of 14 and 16. I have also taken courses and classes in things like Barbizon and H & R Block. I have done these things to keep active, to see what it is that I can do, and to find ways to meet other people. Job wise, it also helps me to see how far I can go mentally without stressing myself out and still enjoy the pleasure of working like everyone else.

One of the best experiences of my life was the chance to learn how to be on my own without my family. This experience was unexpected. I didn't even plan for this experience to come when it did. I was grateful to God for the experience when I had the chance to do it. Through high school, one of my teachers had put my name in for the chance to go to Russia. When I heard about this, I was surprised. It was unexpected that anyone would have thought about me or remembered me while going to this school. I didn't feel like anyone cared about me at all, teachers, students, or counselors alike.

I told my mother and she gave me the okay to go on the trip. The only thing needed was the money, which was a lot. Since it was my trip, I went to my family church. I used my music ability and my family to raise money to help me to go on this trip. After the program, when I was home, I read the cards and counted the money. I then sent thank you cards to everyone in return.

Years later, I found out that my grandmother had secretly given a lot of money in order for me to go on the trip. Instead of it making feel happy, it made me feel angry because I felt that I couldn't thank her in the same way as everyone else. To me, my grandmother had been too proud to tell me during the time of the event, and had waited until during an argument to tell me. So, if she had to wait that long to tell me, to show her that I was growing up, I didn't thank her, but not because I didn't want to. I wanted my grandmother to stop being so proud and acting as if I couldn't handle information.

Through this whole experience, I again had a chance to work on my social skills. I met a lot of other kids my age. During orientation time, I had the chance to meet special people and go to special places. I went to the Capitol and met Senator Paul Sarbarnes. We also had a tour hearing about the history of Washington, DC. The next day, we then left to go to Russia. I was on for both my first trip out of the country and for the chance to prove to my family that even with my condition, I could still take care of myself without them.

Having the chance to go on the three-week trip to Russia was an adventure for me. This trip made me feel like a "big-little" person in one. I felt "big" because I had this big title in my name as well, Student Ambassador of the United States. It made you feel like those old people that you see all the time on the news coming to see the President of the United States. More importantly, I felt "big" because I was away from my family for the first time. This was even the first time that I had been on a plane.

# CHAPTER 4

## A SURPRISE TURNS INTO A DREAM

While in Moscow, we went on a tour where we took a lot of pictures. Experiences also occurred with the Black Market where people would come up to you and sell things that usually weren't good for you. While there, we visited the Lenin Mausoleum, which was worshiped like a religion. There we stayed at the Molodehmaya Hotel for one night.

In Moscow, we also went to the Moscow Kemlin where a group of churches was set in a square. After this visit, we went back to the hotel. While at the hotel, I took a nap and later that day, we left on the train to go to Leningrad, our next stop.

On July 23, 1990, we arrived in Leningrad after a very nice train ride. Here in Leningrad, the experience was the opposite of the experience in Moscow. The food was better, but the tour in Leningrad wasn't as good as the one in Moscow.

The sites in Leningrad that we saw during the tour were very sad. However, we went to see Swan Lake, a ballet production, at the theater on the next day, July 24, 1990. We went on a tour to the Petrodvocets (which is another name for Peter's Place). When we toured Peter's Place, we had to wear slippers to protect the floor of the place because everything was kept in perfect condition.

We visited a place to see where Russian music was made and while there, I had a chance to play on their grand piano. The rest of the day was spent relaxing with some of the people I met on the trip.

On July 25, 1990, the day was spent in relaxation. After breakfast, time was spent looking for gifts to take back home. That afternoon, we went to a museum called the Heritage, which had a lot of pictures in it. After going to the museum, we came back to the hotel, ate dinner, and prepared to go to a social. At the social, I was able to give out some of the gifts I had from the United States, which we were told to bring with us.

While there, I received a gift from a soviet named Cauiu. I had a nice time at the social talking to Cauiu, despite the social barrier. He was a very nice person, and I tried to teach him the electric slide. In return, he gave me one of their musical instruments.

Our next stay was at Novgorad on July 26, 1990. Getting there was difficult because the bus was not working correctly. Once we arrived in Novgorad, the day was spent getting settled. The rooms in the hotel were so nice that they made you feel like you were at home. My stay in Novgorad wasn't as nice as it could have been because I had a lot of seizure attacks, which caused me to feel tired and then unable to eat.

While there, a tour was taken of Novgorad where we saw very pretty churches. A visit was also taken to the Yurien Monastery. After lunch, we attended a nice concert, and the rest of day was spent resting.

July 28, 1990, the next day, wasn't very exciting. A drive was taken to see a bell factory early in the morning. The visit wasn't what was expected. There was nothing in it that pertained to bells. During the ride, a majority of us slept on the way. Later, time was spent shopping, and I was able to find gifts for my family. Later in the day, we took a boat ride. The scenery during this boat ride wasn't great, which made it very boring.

That evening, we went to a Russian disco during our free time. A Russian disco you can picture as an American disco. The difference is that their disco is held outside where there was a very bad scent. This scent carried everyone's body odor as if it were in a closed room.

The next day, while still in Novgorad, was a very slow-moving day. We spent the morning sleeping in. In the afternoon, we went to the Kremlin. Afterwards, time was spent getting ready for our departure to Kalinin.

On July 30, 1990, we left for the city of Kalinin. When we arrived, we ate lunch in Vyshni Volockok, which had some nice food. I wasn't feeling well because the day before, I had eaten food that made me feel sick. Lately, I hadn't eaten any fresh vegetables. During our stay in Kalinin, we met really nice people who greeted us on the bus. We were greeted by our host families. In my host family, the mother's name was Demaia, the father's name was Victor, the grandmother's name was Nastia, the sister's name was Olga, and they had a daughter named Tamara. After meeting them, we were greeted by the mayor of Kalinin with bread and salt.

After meeting the mayor, I left to stay with my host family. We left with a crazy fast driving cab driver. My host family had a beautiful house in the country. They were a very nice family. It made them feel really good when we tried to speak in their Russian language.

One of the ladies who went with us on the trip came with me. Her name was Miss Holland. A grand meal was made for us when we (Miss Holland and I) arrived at their house. The host family takes it very personally if you don't eat a lot of the food made for you.

After dinner, a walk was taken around the village, which had a lot of rocks in it. Being with the host family made me feel as if I were at home. My family had two homes. The other home was a flat in the city. We went there the next day.

On July 31, 1990, my host family took us on a ride on a Russian bus. This was the first time I had ever been on a Russian bus. We went to a local museum, which showed old teapots like some of the ones my father used. I also saw really old cloth and how the cloth was made. We were also shown how people lived in a model type home that was built in the museum. Afterwards, we spent time again in stores where I was able to find some more souvenirs. I also started to spend more of their Russian money (which wouldn't be any good to me at home except as a souvenir).

We ate lunch at the Volga restaurant later on, where some of my friends were staying. We then took a boat ride to my family's flat. We also had to ride another crazy taxi on a crazy street, which made you feel as if you were going to die. Afterwards, I spent the rest of the day relaxing because I felt really tired. Everyone else spent time doing another activity that evening. I was too tired to participate.

On August 1, 1990, breakfast was eaten with the host family. Since there was free time open, it was spent going into town to shop. Later, a tour was taken of the city. Lunch was eaten at a hotel where they usually had meat and potatoes. Everyone in our group was getting sick of eating the same food constantly. After lunch, our group visited a church that happened to be stuffy. We were allowed to ask the priest questions. I personally didn't stay in the church very long because it was too stuffy for me.

After the visit to the church, Miss Holland and I went back to have dinner with the host family.

A day of sadness came for me. August 2, 1990, was the last full day with a very nice host family. The stay was a very nice, fun, and exciting experience. On this day, a tour was held of some very small sights in Kalinin. We also had been learning new Russian words. An example of a Russian word is "Ducha," which means a group of houses that are in the country.

That evening, a fun time came that made the day seem better. Later in the evening, a picnic was held in the woods with our host families if you were lucky to have the chance to stay with one. This was a chance to say goodbye. Conversations and gift-giving was held with our families. They had given us gifts and in return, we did the same. I had received pictures of them as a gift. I also received a Russian flag from them.

August 3, 1990, signified the last meal with my host family. The breakfast was very quiet. The father of the home went to get Miss Holland and I a cab. When you think about the cab drivers over there, you think fast. Then we had another fast ride with a cab driver. This particular cab driver had to dodge some dogs in the middle of the road by driving on the curb. When we arrived back to meet everyone else, we settled on a bus that took us to visit a local television studio.

At the television studio, we answered question about our stay and our thoughts of Kalinin. One of the questions I answered because it related to staying with a host family. After the tour of the television studio, we went back to the hotel. We then ate lunch before getting ready to leave for home.

On the bus, I spent time catching up on my writing and reading. On our trip back to Moscow, I spent time sleeping. Everyone else also spent time sleeping on the trip back to Moscow. When we arrived in Moscow, we stayed at the same hotel—the Molodezhmaya Hotel—where we'd stayed when we arrived in the USSR. We ate dinner at the hotel. The dinner was great, even though others didn't think so. This ended our day going to our last city.

On August 4, 1990, breakfast wasn't satisfying to me. I also didn't feel like eating a lot of food. While in Moscow, we visited a Novodevicki Convent, which wasn't satisfying to most of us in the group. Things started to look alike. In that same area, we went to the Beriozka Shop. The items in the shop were costly. It made you feel upset that you would have to pay a lot for the items. Later on, we had lunch in the Arbat area and a tour. Time was spent in the Arbat area buying items to help us to get rid of our rubles. (Rubles are the Russian form of money.) We needed to get rid of them because we could not get them changed back to the American money.

It's very hard to spend and get rid of Russian money, especially if items are very high priced. The Russians will take our American money, but have no way of giving it back if you are leaving.

After dinner, we went to a Moscow Circus. When compared to an American Circus, it may not look as good. If you forget about America and its circus, it doesn't look bad if you go with the intention of experiencing something new. I looked at the circus as if I lived in Moscow. This helped make the circus really nice to see.

On August 5, 1990, an experience that was supposed to take place didn't. We were to go to a student camp, but had gotten lost. Directions were asked of a policeman who told us that we would run into a military installation camp and could get arrested. So, a long trip of 60 miles was wasted.

After lunch, some people went to a museum or to the Beriozka Shop for a few minutes. After returning, we had free time that was spent playing cards.

That evening, we ate dinner at the hotel before we left to go to a café. At the café, we socialized with some more Soviets, I expected the type of people to be my age, but they were older.

When we went back to the hotel, I spent the rest of the day writing and talking to Miss Cassidy and Mrs. Hayes, who were two other teachers in the trip.

The rest of the time I spent resting and writing in my book. Our group was feeling a lot of emotions. The time was drawing near for us to get ready to go back home to the United States.

The day called the Last Day finally arrived. We left on August 7, 1990. To be on time for our plane ride, we woke up at 4:00 a.m. This didn't help at all. We didn't get out on time. We were the second bus to get on Aeroflat, which is a really small plane that is very hard to move around in. The comfort of a Russian plane is not the same as the comfort of an American plane.

After our flight to Germany, we were checked out again. I personally had scissors in my bag that would make traveling for me difficult. The scissors had to be packed separately from me and I was to receive them later in New York. We also had other problems as well. There was a layover problem and a missing child, which caused us to wait at the airport longer than we expected. While at the airport, we also had a quick lunch.

After some time, we were able to get on the plane to New York for the John F. Kennedy Airport.

This ends my whole experience, which was a surprise to me. I was able to see other parts of the world and experience life differently for myself. I had also received Soviet pins from people that I had met as souvenirs for visiting their country. Pictures were also taken of the nice places that I had visited during my stay in Russia. I had fun times with those whom I had met in my group, whether it was during one of the activities or the relaxing times we had together doing things like playing cards.

Personally, I learned through this trip that I would be able to take care of myself despite my condition. It gave me the chance to see and live life in a different way. This trip gave me a surprise that I had never really focused on for myself. The most special thing that this surprise gave to me was where it led. This surprise led to my dream. The dream was "My Prom."

My trip gave me a way to fulfill my dream of going to my prom. I was a person that didn't have many friends. I didn't have the connections that most girls have in knowing someone who would like to take them to their prom. If I were to go, I would have been going by myself or not at all. However, due to my trip, I was brought into contact with other students.

It was now time for my dream to come true. This dream, you could say, is second in line with getting married. Surprisingly, you don't forget this day.

The only people that I knew at this time were those that I had just met from going on my trip to Russia. I was scared when I took this chance. I took the list of names and dialed the first male guy on the list. His name was Carlos. I was nervous when I picked up the telephone to call him. I had also pictured myself having to dial every guy on the list. Thank God I didn't have to do that. God had made my date the first name on the list.

When I called, I was lucky that Carlos was home. I asked him if he would escort me to my prom, which was to be held on May 17, 1991. I was surprised when Carlos said, "Yes." Personally, I wasn't expecting much from him. I was just so happy to have someone to escort me.

Before the prom, I went shopping with my mother. I purchased an emerald green dress with matching shoes and diamonds. (The emerald is my birthstone.) Just before the day of the prom, I had my hair and nails done.

On the day of the prom, Carlos arrived and to my surprise, he came with a limousine. I was astonished to see the limousine. The way that I felt, you could have taken me in anything. I didn't see myself as that special. That is how he had made me feel. I felt like a special girl on a special night. You could have matched my emotions up with those of Cinderella. He also had a corsage for me. When we arrived at the prom, those in my class were surprised by the nice guy I had with me. They probably didn't think that I would have anyone with me at all, by the expressions on their faces.

At the prom, we danced and took pictures, as well. (The picture sits out in the living room and every time that I see it, I admire it.)

This day, the prom, was the end of a bad past and the beginning of a good future.

# CHAPTER 5

## BACK TO SCHOOL

When I went to high school, "except for the trip to Russia" it turned out to be the worst four years of my life. Nobody in my family, I believe, had any faith in me. Even if you talk to some of them today, seven or more years later, they still say the same things. I had gone to an all-girl high school. Every year, I hoped and believed for the same things. I wanted, of course, good grades, friends, my emotional pain to stop, and—most of all—for the seizures to stop.

I may have gotten decent grades, but nothing else would follow through for me. Things just got worse.

At St. Ann's High School, the homework was tough. People I knew did not have conversations with me. They did not understand why I would do so much homework. The homework at this school kept me up studying until 10:00, sometimes 11:00 p.m. My school gave out that much work. Our school had a nine-period day. Three of the periods were lunch, study hall, and gym. Having a seizure disorder made it difficult to hold in information like the average person. I had to study far in advance. I could not study in one night, as most people do, because it would just make me nervous and stress me out even more. So, I just put up with it and planned my time out well to get through it all.

The teachers in the school were difficult. I had to find ways to get around them because sometime they acted as if they did not want to answer your question. There are teachers who will make you question your grades. Music class is an example because the teacher had to go by personal judgment. Music was a class that did not give homework or tests.

My emotions seemed affected because I still could not get what I wanted. I wanted the teasing to stop and to have some friends in my class, like everyone else. I still could not win because people continued to tease me. When I had gym with my classmates, it became a lot worse than when I was in grade school. I thought that I could have a better chance, at least with those who did not know me that well, but that did not happen at all. The only time that I could make any friends was during my lunch period with students who were not in my class. I was still miserable inside because I had to be around those who were in my class a lot more.

Physically, this was a stressful time as well. I was praying a lot during this time for my seizures to stop. But, in fact, I was having them more often. I would have them at school, on the bus, or just anywhere possible.

Nobody in my family believed that I could do anything with this disorder. Some were even against me attending a private or Catholic school. My family saw how hard I would work and that it would cause me to have the seizures, maybe because of the physical stress. All I wanted at the time was for my doctors to make the seizures stop.

It was just important to me that I finish no matter how it made me feel. If it meant that for four years, I lived on six to seven hours of sleep five days a week, then this is what I did.

I have never received a 3.0, much less a 4.0 average. However, through it all, I still learned something because it prepared me for my college life. It made me feel mentally stronger inside. When I got to college, my first goal was to plan out my schedule to fit my mental, emotional, and physical life. While I was in St. Ann's, I had no choice but to do what others told me to do.

# CHAPTER 6

## THE BEST TIME OF MY LIFE (COLLEGE)

The best time of my life has been my college life. During my time in college, I was able to live a different life. This life allowed me to feel like a totally different person. I could put my past emotions behind and become a totally different Macena. Whoever I was before, I felt, no longer existed. I had small experiences that seemed big because I had never experienced them before, experiences that give people the chance to relate with each other.

The most special experience for me was just in making friends. That has been the hardest trial that I could ever accomplish. While in college, I was able to have friendships with people by joining clubs. This led to me being able to learn, feel, and know that I could form the relationships with people, which I had always had a hard time making.

The relationships that I have made with people allowed me to learn that there are people out there in the world who will care for you. In college, I had different experiences with my emotions. These emotions consisted of someone wanting to be with you and /or you just wanting someone to be a part of your life as a friend.

In college, I experienced relationships with guys that I had never experienced before. One was the simple thing of someone just wanting to associate with me constantly. I had never had anyone show such an interest in me as a person. This person, Mark, loved to be around me. He loved having talks and called me often. He also had the same condition as I did. What made us different is that he lived his life like there was nothing wrong, even though mentally, he was very smart and educated about what was wrong. He didn't want to take the medication, but always expressed happiness easily. All of this went on during the time that I knew him, until it all caught up with him. He ended up dying from his seizure disorder. This really hurt me because it felt as if he were being punished for not admitting to himself that he had a disorder.

Throughout my time in college, I also made friends through the clubs I joined. This allowed me to find a way to open up differently with others. The club activities were put together in ways to allow us to express ourselves. In the Republican Club, I met people that I became close to, knowing and doing outside activities with them.

Outside of school, there were times when we would get together just to have fun. I would sometimes be invited to go out for activities like church, picnics, and even to have study dates. Rarely did I have people in my life that remembered me as I would remember other people who were special to me—like my college friends remembering my birthday by giving me cards and chocolate cake one year.

One experience that I rarely expected but have constantly thought about was that of having someone in my life. For me, this experience was very hard, emotionally. Even when given the chance, I couldn't express myself as completely as most girls had by this time in their lives. Personally, it made me feel as if I would always be a step behind. This is a step that I may never catch up to. Even if I did get close to it, it would never be or feel complete.

I personally didn't know what it would feel like to have someone want to be with me. Even if you couldn't put in your 50% of the relationship, they were willing to keep trying. For me, it was difficult to express myself in a close emotional relationship when I have always felt one way because of how people saw me as a person. I could only dream about it.

I had my chance at the relationship in college with someone I will name Tony. It was very difficult. I personally had a hard time accepting the words "I love you" from someone's mouth who didn't look like me. Expressing myself emotionally, even sexually, is difficult. It's like being a baby in an adult suit. I am a person who never learned how to open up to other people.

Special times have occurred outside of school as well. One was the chance to perform in the Christmas program to play a classical Christmas song. I was asked by Myrna Summers, a professional singer herself, who attended my church (the Refreshing Spring Church Of God in Christ). Unexpectedly, she asked me to perform the song early in the year. I accepted the chance to perform. I practiced the song all year up to the Christmas program, which was held at my church.

I also had invited family members to come, but this didn't turn out as I wanted it to. The song, when performed, didn't turn out right because my emotions were broken. I was hurt because I didn't see any of the family members that I'd asked to come. Since I felt hurt inside, it messed up the song.

The chance to perform will always be treasured. The picture of how I dreamed it to be was not how it turned out. It made me feel as if I disappointed someone because I wasn't pleased with myself. So, I felt that I owed Myrna Summers an apology. I will never know if she was really angry with me. I know that if I were, I might have been disappointed. That is how I felt about myself.

Other programs that I have done had nothing to do with music. The programs related to ballet when I was taking dancing classes. This, for me, was another way to express and show myself emotionally. It also gave me the chance to meet other people.

These experiences during different times in my life helped me grow and gave me a chance to be a part of a group. I was never the person who could speak openly very easily to other people. So, other ways had to be found to get me closer to people to practice what I had never learned how to do as a child. What people don't realize is that social skills are just as hard to learn as sitting in class and having the teacher instruct you.

We all have different things in which we excel. Sometimes, those areas have to be used to assist in learning what you don't know. We all need to have people in our lives. These relationships come in the form of families, friendships, or work relationships. A lot of times, one relationship helps form another. You need to hold faith in yourself to help you learn and achieve goals in creating relationships. A lot of the emotional pain that happened in grade and high school seemed to have stopped. A lot of my dreams seemed to come true. What my counselors in high school seemed to think about Prince George's Community College is not true. They did not give it the credit that it deserved. Going there was great because a lot of my prayers finally came true.

My first prayer was to find some really good friends and to be a part of some club activities. My second prayer was to get a really good counselor that would understand me. Throughout the five years that I spent at the PGCC, I received a total of three awards, called Minority Student Retention Awards. Both students and counselors can receive these awards. The student answers a questionnaire about the relationship and the job the counselor does for the student.

Nothing like this took place in high school. I am surprised that some of my prayers were heard. I also received help in other areas in my life to make things go a little easier.

Going there felt really comfortable because my father worked there. I went to school there on the work program for their workers. The only requirement that the school has is that the student passes the classes. Personally, I did not mind trying to pass my classes. I was already a hard worker. Tuition was due for the class if the student did not complete or pass the course.

While going there, I did come into a little setback during my second quarter. I had a series of bad epileptic seizures, which lasted the whole entire week of Easter Vacation. It turned out to be the worst Easter I had ever had. While at church, I was walking in front of the pews during the offertory and all of a sudden, I had an attack. Every day for the whole Easter week, I had an attack.

When I went back to school, I went into the computer room to try to work on the computer. All of a sudden, a feeling of blankness or emptiness came over me. Physically, I knew that I had been taking computer classes because I had the proof, the computer books.

Mentally, I could not recall the correct information to help me to perform the work. Recalling information from January to April was very difficult. The loss of information upset me. I began to cry.

My life after that seemed to become a big mess. I started having to live my life out of notebooks, pens, and pencils because I just could not trust my brain as everyone else could. If I do not have it in a second location, more likely than not, I am not going to remember it.

Every week, seven days apart, for a whole year when I was in school, I had seizures, regardless of the fact that I was still on my medication. While in school, I had to do a lot of re-reading of material because every time I would get sick, I would forget the information. So, I read the information before the teacher taught it, then again after an attack, and then once more before my exam.

To keep me happy, I also kept journals, or diaries, of my life to help my memory as well. It has always been depressing to me that I could not remember what has happen to me. To help me feel good about myself, I began to write down the many good times so that I could remember how good my life has been.

During my time in college, I joined two clubs just to meet people. Guess what? It worked. It helped to open me up some. While I was in school, it made me feel good about myself.

The first club that I was in was the Starship Toronto Club during my first semester. I did secretarial work for this club. The next club that I was a part of was the Republican Club, which dealt with Republican activities. We also had a fashion show to raise money for the club. I did secretarial work for this group as well. I received a Certificate of Service Award from the college for the service gave to these clubs.

In December 1996, all of this had to come to an end. It was time to graduate. I graduated with an Associate of Arts Degree in Microcomputers. In a way, I was both happy and sad. I was happy because I had achieved my goal, but sad because the fun that I had at the school had come to an end. I had really enjoyed myself with the atmosphere of the people and the surroundings. I had not felt emotionally stressed as I had in high school. Now, it was time for me to push for my working and personal goals.

# CHAPTER 7

## FAMILIES, FRIENDS, & CHILDREN WITH DISORDERS

### Families

Families do not realize that when they do not support their child in whatever they do, they could be hurting that child. People do not realize how sensitive the word "Yes" can be. When you say it out of the air, you do not know whether someone believes you or not. You do not know whether that person knows to believe you. You, as a family member, have to learn to be careful about what you say that you are going to do. You could be building up someone's self-esteem one day and dropping it the next.

Families also have to support the child by giving the child the information it needs in order to survive in the real world. The protection or decision-making made by parents because of their own personal experiences may not help the child grow up, or it may cause the child to grow up at a much slower rate.

Families need to take the time to learn about the disorder and spend time talking to the child more. Families also have to learn to accept some of the decisions the child may make as an adult about his or her own disorder. Once the child begins to grow up, family members should begin to acknowledge this. Once the child becomes an adult, they should no longer be treated as a child.

My personal family has put me through emotional stress. This is just as bad as having the seizure disorder itself. It is much like having two disorders at one time. This is not right. Nobody has the right to put emotional stress in anyone's life.

## Friends

Friends can be a good support system to the child-even if the person is a young adult—and to the family. Friends can help keep the family in line and from falling apart. Families tend to fall apart when they have to deal with a big responsibility. This is where the support of a friend comes in. The friend can help the family get the information it needs and just help in giving extra love whenever the family needs it.

Family friends may know other people who know about the disorder. Those people can also become friends of the family as well.

Friends can be more impartial because they are outside of the direct family unit; therefore, they can help keep up the spirits of the family. For this to work, families have to stop being shy about admitting to having a child with a disorder and be willing to allow others into their world. Parents have to allow doctors, teachers, and other family members into this world. You might as well allow friends into this world as well. They usually are not going to do harm to the child. To me, they can be a lot nicer than most family members can, because most family members have already made their decision about you. Your friends have to first understand you before they make their decision about you. This is supposed to happen in the family but usually the child with the disorder is too young to speak up. The damage is done before we can speak for ourselves.

## Children

The child with the disorder should build up their self-esteem to become a strong, organized, and independent adult. Below, I will share some of the things that I personally do for myself. They may be beneficial for others as well.

I want you to find your own ways to focus and to get goals accomplished in your life. You are not going to have your parents or your families to back you up all of the time. Many times, your families are not going to have the time to back you up, so you have to learn how to depend on yourself. After you get into the habit of doing it, it feels so good that you will love to do things for yourself. Do not think that it's because you are becoming a selfish person. You're simply becoming a more independent person.

One thing I do is to make lists for myself. The lists help me when my mind doesn't help me. It helps me to remember and keeps me in line. I also try my best to keep order in my room. That does not mean that my room does not get messy. What it means is that one type of thing stays or goes in one area. I have a whole bunch of folders that are named and separated by subject. I pay my own bills. Bills that have not been paid go in one drawer. Paid bills go in another drawer. I also keep a goal list on my wall to keep me focused on the goals for my life. Every now and then, I read these goals that are over the top of my bed to keep my spirits high.

All of this can build up over time, so I have to plan time to clean out these areas. About every three to six months or so, I clean out certain drawers to keep order in my life.

Whatever you decide to do while you are a child growing into a young adult, do not let your family control all of your decisions. Sometimes, you are going to have to start standing up to them and telling them how you feel. Usually, you should not holler at family. Personally, I do not believe in hollering. But sometimes, families can only comprehend one thing—hollering. I am not saying that makes it right. However, learn to stand up for what you believe in—whatever it is.

The most important thing is not to let your disorder control who you are. You are to do your best in trying to live as much of a normal life as possible. You need to realize that you are a person first before you are a sick person with a disorder. When you speak about yourself, do not talk about your disorder unless it is with someone whom you know is going to be in your life personally for a long time. When getting a job, save it for after they have given you the job so that it will not be an excuse for them not to hire you.

Present yourself as a normal person, but accept that there are still going to be things that you are not going to be able to do like other people. Keep on trying to reach your personal goals. Do not let anyone stop you from trying to reach your goals. Do what makes you feel good and happy. Your family has had its chance to pull their lives together.

Now it's your turn to pull your own life together. To do that means seeing what it is that you can do. Sometimes, you have to go out and test the water in the real world. Just take a chance. A lot of times, you may have to stop asking for other people's permission to do things or you may never get the chance to do what it is that you want to do. There comes a time when you have to start living what is usually considered a dangerous life by your family. For you, it is maturing.

Keep in mind that there are people in the world who may be times 10 worse than you. You could have had another condition that would have made your life like living in darkness. I don't personally know how people who have mental and physical conditions feel on the inside, but I do have a slight idea of it because of knowing someone in my family. He is my cousin, whom I will call Jonathan, and he has Cerebral Palsy, which is both a mental and physical disorder. This disorder has no choice but to put a lot of pain and emotional stress on the parents of the child because the child cannot move for itself.

Keep in mind that you have a seizure disorder, which means that 50% of the time you live like a normal person. Sometimes, it's your family who takes the other 50% away from you. Be happy that you do not have to be a totally dependent person like my cousin. Go out there and get your 50% and more if possible. I personally believe in taking all that I can get. Try to get as close to 100% as you can. You may or may not make it to 100%, but you will do better than those who do not make an effort at all.

# CHAPTER 8

## WHAT ARE EPILEPTIC SEIZURES TO ME?

Epileptic seizures can start on either side of the brain. On the right side or the working side of the brain, a person can have petit-mal (small) or grand-mal (big) seizure. These seizures cause the working side of the brain to turn off. They can also cause the nerves in the body to shake slowly or quickly for short or long periods of time. When I come out of it, I can close my eyes and feel a blank space in my brain. That is very uncomfortable.

To make myself feel emotionally satisfied or happy, I would have to ask someone questions about the seizure and what had happened. An example of this person would be my mother because she knows my body. I would ask at least five questions to feel emotionally satisfied. I would then quickly write the information down to give to my doctor, a neurologist. I have had these seizures off and on in my life.

By the time I was in college, my seizure disorder had become more regular. As regular as knowing that Tuesday came before Wednesday.

Since the attacks I had over Easter Vacation, and due to the severity of their impact on my learning abilities, I had to re-think my whole life and how I was going to function mentally around my seizure disorder—the part of me that always made me feel "low, sad, depressed, angry." I started setting goals for myself to keep my mind mentally focused on what I wanted to do in my life like other people did. I keep these thoughts on top of my bed because "mentally" I lose them and "physically" get "low, sad, depressed, or angry."

I "physically" know in body that I had been working on something or done something, but I don't or can't remember quickly what it is. So, to build me back up again or to find my self-esteem, I quickly go to my awards. I pull these awards out and look at them for few minutes to help my mind remember that I am a "good" person and an "okay" person.

Having a seizure disorder pulls me down because I can't mentally function on a "natural" basis. There are simple things, like smiling, that are hard for me because my emotions are cut off like two wires in a computer that won't stay together. The only time I can "smile" is when I am physically active in speaking for a long period of time. It's not that I have forgotten: my mind won't let me make the physical connection between the emotional and mental part of my brain like those who do not have emotional or mental disorders.

After the bad seizure at church, I began having to use more outside connections to help me feel more mentally comfortable.

Example:

1) Through my vision, I find things that can help me to remember. Example: Finding something common about someone through something that I already like.

2) Write these common things down, like definitions, with their name or mentally repeating it to myself.

3) Write directions down with the names of people or things that I visit or do often. In time, I would start to naturally remember slowly if I don't stress myself out.

4) Remember to write out messages. I remember them naturally better when they are in more than one place.

5) Set focus times for things that I have to do constantly, like taking my medication.

6) Keep calendars to keep my life straight.

7) Keep a goal list on walls to build my self-esteem. Goals can change as often as my life issues change.

8) Write journals about the good things in my life.

9) I now write out the bad things in my life to relieve some of the tension and then throw them away.

10) I now have to prepare mental statements for myself because a mind with a seizure disorder like epilepsy can make you look (in your face), feel, or sound like a person that you are not, if not given the chance to really express yourself.

People don't realize how much of your natural ability is taken away. It's not that you have chosen to become a mentally or physically weak person. It's just that the medications are so strong that they have control of both the inner and outer part of the body. An example is looking at my face in the first 30 seconds. You would assume that I am "sad" but you could be wrong. I could be just as "happy" as you who show a brilliant smile. Don't compare epileptics to people whom you think are "normal" just because they "smile." The expression on the epileptic face could be from the medication and not a true inner feeling at that time.

Over the years, I had to go to a psychiatrist to get some of my emotions out. I wrote letters, not caring if they were answered. The important thing to me was that I had gotten out some of what my mental and emotional mind and physical body couldn't take or hold on to anymore. I wrote letters to people whom I knew had put some pain on me in my life that I felt I couldn't speak to. Sometimes, I couldn't speak to them because I felt that they did not know me as well as they should. I felt that for a first, they should get to know the real me. Usually, there wasn't enough time for me to speak to let out all that I wanted to say because it's hard when your mind keeps on stopping you.

The only thing I did was to write out my thoughts and then mail them to the people whom I felt should know. If they had questions, it was up to them to call me. The important thing to me was that some of my feelings, thoughts, anxiety, and tensions were out of me for the first time without feeling scared or having the struggle of speaking that my epileptic seizure disorder gives to me. If I am unable to get it all out, I become tense inside because of the stress of putting together one good thought or thinking that I am going to get my goal—one goal being able to listen to a general conversation.

Most people, when they meet me, can't get past my face because it looks sad when in reality, I am more of a happy person on the inside. My happiness will come out more when you get to know me and take the time to know me a lot better. This is true with any person with epilepsy or possibly any disorder because of the medication that has to be taken on a daily basis. So, to keep the tension or pain down off of my head, I have to keep a calm look on my face. To you, I could look like a sad person.

Since I could never speak about how I was truly feeling, I mentally tried to block some of the pain away with some of the activities I did. Physically, even if I wanted to, I didn't have the same desire as everyone else to do things like sports. I didn't mind looking at them for a while but physically, they always made me feel drained inside, which caused me to feel down. Personally, I hated that feeling. So, to build up my self-esteem, I started to find and do more activities in the outside world to take my mind off of some of the mental pain that my seizure disorder caused.

When I feel down, I pull out my certificates of things that I have done in my life to help me to internally "smile" again. Up to age 25, I have achieved these goals:

1. Play the piano in concerts and at weddings

2. Graduated from Grade School

3. Learned to ride the Metro bus and train on my own

4. Certificate of Service from Leland Memorial Hospital

5. Certificate of Accomplishment from Youth Bowling Program

6. Prince George's County Police Safety Patrol Award 7. St. Jerome Awards (2) for Religion & (1) for Special Effort

8. Certificate for the World Music Festivals in High School

9. Honor Certificate for Bach Festival

10. Certificate of Recognition from Calvary Alliance Church of God in Christ; Graduated from "St. Ann's"

11. Traveled to Russia as Student Ambassador of United States

12. Certificate of Graduation from Barbizon School

13. Certificate from St. Ann's High School Choir

14. Certificate of Graduation from H & R Block Tax School

15. (3) Certificates of Recognition from Prince George's Community College in the

16. Minority Student Retention Program

17. Certificate of service award from Prince George's Community College

18. Received Associate of Arts degree in Microcomputers from Prince George's Community College

I received some of these awards because of things that I did for other people. Other awards, like those given to me while in college, were given to me on the spot, without my knowing that I would be receiving them.

There was a time in my life that I felt so small that my self-esteem was low. Then I made myself believe or think that anything was possible. I told myself, "I am smart." After receiving these awards, I can now see that it is possible.

My seizure on July 16, 1998, was the worst that any person could ever have—a Temporal Lobe or Psychomotor Seizure. My doctor had changed my medication and I had been very emotional because I had gone on a vacation to California not long after he changed it. I did not know that the medication did not control the emotional part of the brain. So on this day, I had on out-of-body attack, which caused me, without realizing it, to call my mother and do the things that my cat "Peaches" does. When taken to the hospital, I had another attack such that I was fighting with the ambulance driver and others and had taken off my clothes. Later, I started yelling and shaking. Then I was taken and tied down and before I knew it, my body was preparing to scream out my cat's name, "Peaches." I did this for at least three hours.

The whole experience was mentally and emotionally confusing because I would come in and out of it. There were also times when I felt like myself. Afterwards, I became mentally confused because I was in a hospital, but could not figure out the reason. That answer did not become clear to me until all of my thoughts started coming out at me, when I started writing them down on paper. Mentally, physically, and emotionally, I was all backwards for at least seven days. My visual senses had also taken a lot longer to recover because I could feel an uncomfortable pain around my eyes, even though I could still see.

They need to make an effort to sit down and learn about the seizure disorder. People have to realize that all children have feelings and can feel the things that are being thought and said about them. They can also notice the difference in their life when compared to someone else considered normal. No child should be given medication at any age without knowing what the medication is for and why the medication is taken. All children should understand the effects of their own medication. What parents do not realize is that these effects make children appear mentally, physically, and emotionally different than most children. These effects cause children to go through more emotional problems than normal. The child should understand themselves from the beginning about their own lives.

The child should be able to fight off anyone who tries to bother them in different situations. An example is not being fast enough sports games at school. The child would then understand personally that not being fast has nothing to do with their ability. The problem may have more to do with the drowsiness of the medication that they are on for their seizure disorder. There is nothing that they can do about that.

Parents from the beginning need to stop feeling ashamed when they find out that their children have this disorder or any type of disorder. Give your child the same chance as you would your normal child. If you realize it, all the chances you give your normal children, they normally do not want to take them because they know that those chances will always be there for them. I was personally forced to disobey because while I was obeying all of my life, I received no preparation for the outside world.

# CHAPTER 9

## LIVING A BALANCED LIFE: EDUCATIONAL VS. EMOTIONAL

I am writing this chapter to tell people what I believe both emotionally and mentally. All of my life, I have heard people tell me what they have thought was best for me. No one has ever really understood when I tried to tell them what I believed was best for myself. People think that you are too young to know anything about yourself. So, I am going to give you the best clear picture I can about some of my experiences to help you understand life through an only child's eyes—a child who has had a good educational background, but a bad emotional background. (This is the child that has a medical condition.)

What people need to know is that there is both an emotional world and a mental world. Nobody can live in just one world. Everyone, rich or poor, needs both worlds. You need an even balance in your mind with both worlds. The educational or mental world helps to give you the money that we all love so much so that we can get those things like houses, cars, have the children, families, go on trips, etc. The emotional world helps us to express ourselves on paper—smiling, sadness, laughing, joking, enjoying music, pulling our minds together, and enjoying plays. Nobody can really live in one world.

It was my mother and grandmother's decision to send me to a Catholic school because they thought, or at least my grandmother thought, that it would protect me. For that reason, it was wrong.

There are things that I know today that I see that I would not know if I had not gone to a Catholic school, but I do not thank my mother for sending me to Catholic schools for protection because I had no protection. Whether you are in a uniform or not, you still cannot cover a child's mouth and stop a child from wanting to fight. Catholic schools may have more detentions—times when children stay after school for bad behavior—but children still act like children.

If I had gone to a public school, I might not have been as educationally happy as I am today. I may have had the friends, but friends will not get me the jobs or the other things that I need. Some dreams require that you have money. This does not mean that I knock or do not like public schools. I would not have known, at a young age anyway, that I did not learn everything that it was possible to learn in a certain subject. Then I would not have had anyone pushing me to want to study by the amount of homework I had to do every night.

Children who go to public schools have little or no homework to learn many skills. So, I feel blessed by my mother to have had the chance to go someplace to learn as many skills as I did. This does not make me a better person where I could look down on other people who do not have as much as I do. What it does is make me a more helpful person to others. Believe me, if it were possible to get the same degree of work at a public school, then I probably would have gone.

I missed out on the chance from the very beginning to live my emotional life because my family was scared and tried so hard to protect me. My family had the chance to live their personal lives, whether it had been in the family or in the outside world, like in school. I did not have that same chance. My family does not realize how important it is to me to get rid of these feelings. I have to learn how to feel just as strong as they do. The only way that I can do any of that is to get out into the world and to meet other people.

My family may hate the activities that I am trying to achieve, but they are important to me. My family also becomes upset with me when they see me emotionally upset and in tears. However, the only thing that I can do is be patient with myself and break my own cycle of tears, little by little. I can say that I do not cry as hard as I used to. The pain is still intense and I can still get emotional, you may still hear it in my voice, but I may not be screaming as a child would.

Later, your life can also feel very slow because everything around you seems to be happening more often than what you may want. You may find yourself praying. Praying sometimes is the only thing that holds you together. It also makes you feel as if you are going to get what you desire if you are someone who believes in God. That is what I find myself doing. Sometimes, I cannot get things going, so I start to pray. I start hoping that everything will fall into place. What I hate the most is the waiting.

You know how children hate to wait for birthdays to come around? Well, I am impatient about the goals in my life. If I am left to just sit around waiting for dates to come before I can actually put the action to work, it drives me crazy inside. This is only because I feel as if there is time being wasted. I am the type of person who likes to keep their goals on the move. To keep my mind out of the pain that always hurts so badly I keep focused on my goals.

Living a balanced life with my family, especially those around my age, has also been hard on me. People in my family have had this thought that because I am an only child, they believe that I think that I am better than they are. I never thought that at all. Personally, I do not think like that. It is only that my family would not allow me to speak to them when I was little. For a very long time, I could not understand why. People were not being told the right things about me. Sometimes, even today, things are still being told incorrectly and I still do not like it. An example being my grandmother when she tells her stories. She does not realize it, but there are times when she tells the wrong reason for why I may have stopped doing certain activities, especially the ones that she herself loves to do.

The best thing that I can say is that, of the two worlds, whether educational or emotional, neither is better than the other. You need both to survive with yourself and your family.

# CHAPTER 10

## MY BEST FRIEND—MY MUSIC

I wanted something to do, as most kids do, when I was little. I did not choose sports, which is an outside activity. I chose something that I did not know at the time would make me feel mentally and emotionally happy on the inside. I chose playing the piano. When I was six years old, I asked my mother if I could play the piano and she said yes. We found a piano teacher who lived right down the street from my grandmother's house. She was the love of my life. She was a very old teacher, but I loved her to death. She was the very first teacher who introduced me to opera music. Who would have known that I would come to love this music just as much as I love my gospel music? Loving this music has also made me mentally strong with my grandmother because all she could ever think about was "money."

In my life, at the time, I needed something that I could love. I had nobody that I could speak to as a person. My family did not understand me from my point of view. This is why I have held on to my opera music. When I was a child, I was able to get on my piano like others might get on the telephone with friends. I was able to release my emotions. Sometimes, when upset, I did not care about beat or timing. All I wanted to do was to get my emotions out of my system. Truthfully, I never felt 100% better because I wanted to fit in and have the same things everyone had. Yet, this helped me about 50% of the time. So, I ended up doing it a lot.

Through my music, I also learned other music later on in my life, by my choice, of course, when I wanted to. I also learned pop music and gospel music when I played in a church. My first love will always be opera music though, because that is what I started out with and that is what soothes me when I want to be relaxed.

What has always made me happy is the praise I receive when I do my concerts. Doing concerts, either for my old teachers or my new teachers, has always made me feel good inside. The weird thing is that when I am in front of an audience, my whole life changes. I feel like a different person. There are times that I wish that people would treat me the same way that they do after they hear me play on a constant basis, but my pleasure only lasts for that moment. I don't know what it is about my music that makes people treat me so differently. People speak to me and tell me how well I did, but after that initial conversation, it all stops. There are times that I wish for people to see me beyond my music, but to get there you have to speak to me. You also have to give me a big chance to speak to you, too.

The only way I know how to get my emotions out without looking like a big fool in front of people is through my music, when I have the chance. This may be why I always took to it, because it was the only time I knew I would get to be what most people call "popular." In reality, all I really want is to feel the love that I always see people take for granted in their thirty second friendships.

Through my 19 years of music, I have also had the chance to do weddings for people in my family. For me, they were all great occasions to have that chance and honor to be able to do this for my family. In some of the weddings, I have gotten paid for the services that I have done. It was fun having the chance to prepare the music and to learn the wedding song for walking up and back during the ceremony.

I spent some time playing religious music for a church. For a while, it was fun, until I realized that if I hadn't allowed them to stop paying me and doing the service for free, I believe I would have been respected as a regular employee. I couldn't stay after this bad friction, and the church was just a handful of people. I've learned that in order to keep respect, don't give people everything they want just because they are struggling. Sometimes, you have to struggle and be patient.

I cannot lie to you and say that playing the piano is not a great way to make money—because it is. A lot of people have great talent in the music industry, whether it is through playing an instrument or singing. For me personally, it started out as the only way that I could express myself. Then, with my condition, I also feel very comfortable with what it is that I am doing. So, for the rest of my life, I may play the piano for fun at concerts, weddings, and who knows maybe promotional benefits. It will all be my decision and what makes me happy. The same also goes for you. Whatever you choose to do in life, do what feels right to you. The decision may be wrong if it feels like a demand, or a way for someone else to take control of your life. Remember, God did not give all of us the same talents. If he had, this world would be very boring and there would be no need to associate with each other.

# Chapter 11

What I have lived through can be written about in the form of poetry and terms that come from my heart. Everything here is based on my emotional point of view. I hope that you and your children might be able to gain something from this.

**Poem #1**

### A Child Who Can See, But Living Like She's Blind

Don't overprotect me
`Cause I can't see
If you take my dreams away
You may not know what you're doing to me.

We all have a need
To do things like grow
Just like a seed.

If you don't nurture a seed
With water it won't grow
Then an overprotected child
Who hasn't been nurtured won't grow.

So, what's been done to me,
Don't do to your own kids either!!!

**Poem #2**

## A Person That Can't Show

We don't know
How lucky we are
We also don't know
We can go very far.

A lot of the times
It's best not to talk
So others can learn to walk

And that not just in taking steps.
So give people the time they need
You had time to learn to read.
Then you may see all that they can do!!!

## Difference Between Childhood & Adult Friends

Remember, as a person we learn to grow. We start as a baby, then grow to a child, and from there to an adult. We also grow in three different directions. We grow in the order of past, present, and future. The past is our beginning years. The present is our middle years. This is around the time most of us go to college and get married. Lastly, our future is seen in our older years.

Our Childhood Friends can only see you in one perspective. That perspective is as a child, even if you are an adult. You will always be the same person, no matter how much you have changed. They will think of you in the same manner as they did when they were children. Just as your family will. So, if you see your childhood friend, a lot of times it's best to go ahead and let go. Don't fight it if they don't want to speak or be around you anymore. It's because their life has changed. Your life may not move fast enough to keep up with them in their world.

All people, as we get older, want something different. Some people will tell you in words, while others will just leave. Personally, anyone who can't speak to me, in my opinion, has not mentally matured. So, if someone does it to you first, then let go. If you have to let someone go, be a strong person and have a conversation with that person. You may be doing more hurt than good. That person may not see that or feel good about him/herself until years later in life.

An Adult Friend is even more special at times than a childhood friend. Not just because of the years, but because they may get to see and know you in three different ways. First, they will know your past. Your past to them will be an understanding of why you may still be doing things differently. Since they didn't have to see you "live it," all they have to do is "understand it." Understanding someone's past is just as hard. You have to be mentally patient to want to learn it. Next, is the fun part. They get to meet the new you. The person you want to present in this new world doesn't have to show anything from the past, if you don't want to. This is your chance to become an "actor." You can act or play the part of a new person. You can experiment, define, and set goals to become something that is totally different from the old you. This is your chance.

You also have the faith of both yourself and God to get you through it all. So, now you get to act or play the part of the person that you have always wanted to be. Remember, you don't have to change your entire self because there may be things about you that may never change. You will simply have to accept those things. The new adult friends, if they are true adults, will also accept them.

# Chapter 12

## What's Been taken Away?

People do not realize that one can still use their senses, but that these senses can weaken. This can occur when one does not express. Personally, I feel that I have no sense when I am with my family. For example, you use your voice to speak. People use their voices to express an opinion. An opinion to me has always been something good. When I am with my family, it turns out to be something bad. I am not allowed to share or express my opinion as easily as I can when alone. A cycle forms where I feel as if I am going up or down.

Speaking makes it easier to learn. So, when I cannot speak it is hard to learn. Since I started out as a loner, I did not have anyone to converse with or to learn much from when it came to family or the outside world. I can still feel the separation of age and voices of those around me. I can still feel the protection through the words used when one decides to converse with me.

When people do not see me for the age that I am, it is mentally hard on me. When people that you love are involved, it becomes emotionally hard on family members that you have loved for a long time. I found myself going back and fourth with people. This makes me feel as if I have not admitted to myself my true age. Mentally, I really want it all to stop so that I can stay completely steady. I find that it is hard to do when you were use to pleasing a lot of people for acceptance.

Hearing is another example that helps in understanding. If you are not allowed to hear anything, how is one to learn? Hearing and speaking have to work together. You are being spoken to in order to hear.

I always thought that as one got older, more information should be expressed to that person, especially if you knew that person was not getting the proper information. By limiting the amount of information we share with others, we may also be keeping someone out of the family circle.

Families do not realize that talking also has a setback. Talking can cause damage if a person hears the wrong information. Most people should then have the right to defend themselves.

# CHAPTER 13

## MY PERSONAL THOUGHTS

I would personally like to thank you Dr. Jeanette Witter for all that she has given to me. She has given me the chance to do what I could not have done at home. She has given me both a chance and a place where I can express my true feelings. Through her, I was able to learn the difference in the emotions around me and to learn, over time, how to feel good about myself.

Dr. Witter was to me what friends are to others. She gave me her time, place, and most of all, a way to understand myself. She allowed me the chance to be able to feel my feelings and to form confidence. Confidence has been very hard, especially with this disorder. It was hard for me to think good things about myself because I did not have the ability to think good things about myself. I could not do so, not because I didn't want to, but because it was very hard to teach myself to do so. In order for me to think about myself, I needed to be able to remember which is like "seeing". To be able to "see," I needed the ability to "think." I could not "think" good about myself because everything that I "saw" came out as negative, especially when it involved other people.

Since it involved other people, I didn't know how to react or understand. Those whom I knew first, my family, did not know how to teach me because they were scared. This is where Dr. Witter came in; she helped me to understand myself emotionally.

Dr. Witter helped me to "see" myself as a different person and to "think" better of myself. She helped me, over time, to learn how to "love" myself, even with my condition. Learning to "love" myself would have been difficult to learn, especially since I did not have anyone who either had "trust" in me or "felt" that I could be just as good as they were.

Dr. Witter also helped me with the strength that I needed in order for me to have the courage just to want to do something. Courage alone has been a very hard emotion to learn. Where others have both the physical and emotional strength to "do" and to "think" how they want, I had neither. All of my strength was mentally taken by the disorder and physically taken by its medication.

No one could understand me. The only way that one would be able to understand me was if one had taken the time to want to understand me.

No one could understand me. The only way that one would be able to understand me was if one had taken the time to want to understand me. Rarely could anyone, except for someone like my mother, understand me. To understand me, it took a lot more effort. You would have had to give of your time to understand me as a complete person.

What people "saw" wasn't who I really am. I lived my life like half a person, not a complete person. This wasn't my choice. This was the decision made by my disorder, which took away both my ability to think and to feel like I truly wanted to think and feel. This disorder made me feel both sad and angry on the inside; it made me force a particular mental "picture" of my life.

This picture was my mental way of learning how to think better about myself. This picture was made through my goal list. I would think of what I wanted to be and to have in my life. I used this to strive to get what I wanted for myself. I did not want to feel that this disorder had control over me. I forced myself to think good things about my life. How I showed it, is what made my life difficult to live, I could not show it in the same way as those around me.

I lived with a family who didn't know how to trust me—not because they did not want to, but because of their own fears. Through my mother's family's love for me, they internally expressed fear for me. By the time I found out, the damage was done. I didn't know that something was wrong until what I saw had a different appearance. I had only known one emotion, that of love. This emotion made the whole world look perfect. It didn't break until I went to school. My name felt like it belonged more to someone I loved but to whom I could not give love to in return.

My name comes from my father—who is Raleigh T. Mason. My name comes from his nickname, which is Maceo. Whenever I would hear myself say my name, I felt a love for my father. This love wasn't complete in the beginning. Over time, I began to hate myself because I had no emotional comfort from my father. The name made it worse because I kept on seeing what I could not have, which was a father. There were times that I wished I had a different name. I would wonder if my life would have been different if I had been named something else or if I had had a totally different relationship with a different father. Since neither was possible, I slowly dropped the love that I felt for my father. It hurt me to think about what I could not have as a child, which was a loving and caring father. When my feelings began to build, I started to feel again the feeling of wanting a father in my life. This, for me, was the beginning of a new relationship.

There was a chance for a new relationship around the time that I entered college. Surprisingly, this was not just a chance for a new relationship, it was also a time for a new bond to begin as well. It started after I had found out that I would have to go Prince George's Community College. What had felt bad in the beginning, began to feel good instead. What was made to sound bad, made me feel happier in the end. These were all of the gifts that I had never known but that could be mine and would become special awards.

This relationship brought me the chance, not just to have a father, but also to know my father for the first time. To start, I was surprised during the first year of my college life was to know where my father worked. I knew that he was an engineer, but I didn't know where this so-called "office" was located. I was able, for the first time, to relate his job to the college, instead of to an office building. Just because for the first time, I was able to do with him what I had always from the beginning been able to do with my mother. This was to be able to have both a place and people that I could relate to him, personally. I was also able to receive from my father the chance of having a new personality. This was something that I had never expected. This personality, which looks small, felt big to me. The only reason it felt this way is because I had never seen myself as this person. This person is a person everyone has knowledge of and cares to relate to. I went to school for the first time feeling welcome. This small feeling made me feel as if I were "popular." The feeling was deep and it came out big.

I also received from my father the actual time to learn just how to be able to relax whenever I saw him. This I was able to do on territory that didn't belong to him or to me. I was able to have, through school, the time to learn how to slowly want to love my father. It was at this time that I was able to "see" my father as a different person than what I had personally known. What I saw, I began to slowly like and want to relate to myself I could say that for the first time, my name started to have meaning. I don't mind living with it anymore.

So, as you can see, it has been hard work just putting in and getting used to just knowing and feeling for my father. This one step alone has been a hard step to accomplish. I now feel that I will be able to accomplish the next step, which is to bond with my father on different territory. This will then make the picture I have of my father come out even more complete. This bond is called a relationship.

This ends my personal thoughts of my past, which can now move on to the future.

# CHAPTER 14

## THE PAIN IS NOW GONE

I can finally say for the first time that the pain that I have lived through is finally gone. It has been a hard road just trying to be "Macena," and trying to figure out who "Macena" is supposed to be. It has been terrifying to know that the word "best" didn't have the same meaning for me as it did for other people. What was considered my "best," whether physical or mental, had the possibility of coming out looking "poor." Even if I did not come out looking, acting, performing, or even sounding like others, what I did was of my best ability.

All of my mistakes, which may have looked small to others, actually felt really big. They felt this way because nothing that I have tried to do would make it go away. It was never because I didn't want to look, act, or be a better person. It is because I didn't have the "tools" necessary to "allow" me to make that choice from the very beginning. So, decisions that others have been able to make from Day 1, I could not have made until now. It looks late to the world, but for my "world," it is the perfect time for me.

It has always hurt, from the beginning of time, in knowing that I was more of a "betting" tool, that which people used to protect themselves from losing. From first grade on up, it has been hard living with the thought that when I played with others, there would always be that feeling of being left out. This feeling later took place in other areas of my life, as in my family. It has always hurt that good enough was never going to be enough, so I felt that I had to become and look "perfect." Trying to be this way is very hard, especially if there is nobody around to teach or tell you what is wrong without getting upset with the time that it is taking you just to learn one skill. Everyone compared how fast they could do things to what I could do, and not how hard I was trying to do it.

I am grateful that one pain will end. Though the struggle over the hump will now begin, it will lead to a new life.

# CHAPTER 15

## WHY I AM, WHO I AM

Have you ever thought about or said this phrase to yourself millions of times, as a person: "Who am I?" Well, I've done this millions of times because I didn't feel like a person. All of my life, I have had the desire to change. The word change has a variety of meanings such as make or become different, put-on different clothes or fresh coverings, and lastly, the one we all know, the one that deals with money.

Change is a very unique word. It is neither easy nor hard. The word change is also a foreign word because there is no particular one way or answer for how something is to be done. Example, you could be a person who does things on a particular day. You may make the decision to go shopping only on Saturday. So, whenever you want food, clothes, or bank money to start, you do all of this on Saturday. You could also be a person who either does these things on the weekdays or just when you need them. Of all the ways listed, there's no particular right way. You may choose the way comfortable to you because you may work at home, outside of home, or you may not work at all. You just choose the way that is suitable for you and that makes you happy.

The word change is also a word that defines who you are as a person. The word change has an effect on how other people see you as a person. You could be a person who makes so many changes that when people get to meet you, it's very hard. You could be a person that when you make a change, it's not long before you decide to make another one. You could be a person who makes constant changes because you are always running away from situations that are either hurtful or uncomfortable. You may not know how to live through and make the best of a bad situation.

Just because things don't look perfect or fall in your direction quickly, your quick to leave because you think that when someone meets you, they would be quick to judge you.

The word "change" has an effect on another word. This word is the word that means "to be sure of oneself or self-confident, bold, trustful, and confiding." This word is also just as hard of a word as the word change. The word confident is built on the word people, places, or things. As a person, we tend to get our confidence from either the people we know or see, the places we visit, or the things that we do. What makes you the unique person that you are comes from your achievements or the things that you personally achieve for yourself and the things that I know and have myself achieved over a period of time. These achievements have given me my confidence. These achievements are named "My Personal Goal List' or just "Goals" for short.

The word "goal" has a special meaning too. The word can be used anywhere in life. The word can be used in work, play, or personally with yourself to start. Goal, for me, an achievement through effort. So, "My Personal Goal List." is a list of those achievements that have taken a lot of effort for me to achieve. Those things that you may have received or done with a blink of an eye have been achieved, for me, by setting goals for myself.

During the first few years of my life, I grew up feeling like a nobody. I grew up as a person looking at and seeing people doing things that I wanted to do and achieve. I would see people talking with each other and saw many different personalities, which looked like they could become mine. I constantly saw and heard of activities that others were participating in. So, whenever I heard a name, an activity was never far behind. Marie could have been the musician of the family; Johnny could have been the six-foot basketball or football player of the family. Whenever I heard my name, which wasn't very often, nothing ever came right behind it. So, when I started to grow up, I waited for someone to "put" or "teach" something that I could call my own. I waited months at a time.

I was raised to respect adults and treasure them for what they knew, but after some time, I got tired of waiting for someone to make my identity. So, I made the decision, which was hard, to step over the boundaries and make my own identity. If no one was going to do it for me, I would do it for myself. At least, the name "Macena" would have the identity that I wanted it to have. So, the picture of myself would not have to carry the names of everybody in my life. A lot of me would be made by me.

I modeled from everyone around me the picture I wanted to make. I would look at people and place the image of them on myself. I would practice whatever they were doing with myself. If when I practiced the image, it didn't feel comfortable, it didn't make it on my list as a possible image to achieve. So, I carried a lot of personal, emotional, mental, and physical images around with me that could make up the person named "Macena."

The first goal that I achieved would be that I would find something I liked within someone else and make it my own. So, if there was something that someone else did and I could imagine myself doing it and it looked like something I could enjoy doing, then I would decide to try to do the activity for myself. This goal (first goal) would be my music. Most people who know me know that I play the piano. They also know that I play classical music. However, they don't know what made me start playing the piano, or any number of the other things that I do. Yet, there are many people that helped me in achieving my goals.

Growing up, I wanted someone to speak to. I wanted to be someone that someone would be proud of and admire when they spoke to me. Everyday that I went to church, I would notice a lady who received all this attention. Every Sunday after church, everyone walked up to this lady and spoke to her. They always thanked her, smiled, and talked about her constantly. This lady played the piano. Her name was Marie. When I saw her play, I saw that it would give me those things that I desired. It would give me happiness, a way to socialize, and a feeling of knowing that I could "do" or "achieve."

My mother found a piano teacher for me–"Mrs. Lemons. Mrs. Lemons was an old, sweet lady who always carried a smile on her face.

She was also a very patient lady. So, if you made a mistake it didn't bother her at all. The first thing that she taught me was very special because it showed the closeness of a teacher to her student. She placed her hand over mine and placed my right thumb on the most important note in music. That note was "Middle C." When she did this, I felt myself say, "I can do it!" After she did this, I then received my first piano book. This was a black and white book called *The Primer to the Primer Method* by John Brimhall. The first two songs that I learned in this book, which always remind me of her, are "Up We Go." I can say that what she taught me was my first love for music (which happened to be classical).

At this time, I have another teacher who has taught me the science of music. Mr. Earl Hargrove has a degree in music. His "love" for music comes in a different way. He is the one who taught me my major and minor chords. I know that the major of "A Minor" is "C Major." I also learned my one, four, five, and five-seventh chords from him. It is through him that each note that I play, to this day, has special meaning. So, the notes in the songs that I play have special emotion.

He helped me to make a song that was written by someone else to become mine. He helped me to believe in myself He made it possible for me to set goals with my music. Yearly, he would put me into concerts with other musicians. I personally hated the fact all of my life that I couldn't remember anything. As a teacher, he was always thinking ahead. He had the patience with me to take small steps. He knew how much I hated my memory because I could recall few things on my own. He had no problem with being patient with me. To him, achievement wasn't the amount in how much you did, it was how well you did something. He would help me to memorize at least two songs a year. He would help me to do a pair of lines at a time. He even gave me games to play to help me to memorize my music. These games were to mock my music. I was to play one line of music with one band while the other hand just went over the keys. I did this with both my right and left hand. I also learned how to play my music with my eyes closed. This one was my favorite.

My father is another special person who helped me. Through my father. I learned a skill that I treasure to this day; the mental ability to fix objects around the house. To this day, I can understand directions in order to put things together. I will always love my father for this skill.

Another special person in my life is one of my grandmothers. Her name is Shirley Young. Through her, I have learned those skills that help to make you a person. She has taught me how to cook, clean, sew, make special items like rugs, potholders, and taught me games that I play to this day, like cards and puzzles. She also gave me the desire to think of others and to help them. I also learned her special skill-antique collecting.

My father's mother, Pearl Mason, is another grandmother also special to me. From her, I learned what certain emotions looked like. The thing that I learned from her is what love looks like. She taught me how to love others for who they are and not what they can do.

She also taught me how to love people whether or not they are bad or good. She taught me how to love myself. To this day, the skills that deal with people can be put together as one. Both grandparents each taught half of the skill to the best of their ability.

My aunts worked with me to give me those skills that help a person shine. Two of my aunts taught me the ability to be tough. One aunt taught me how to ignore the pain and the other taught me how to believe in myself. They are Elizabeth Williams and Rita Roberts. Two other aunts—Sandra Mason and Denise Young—taught me how to achieve whatever I wanted and to stand tall. Another aunt, Renee Young, taught me how to feel beautiful. And my aunt, Kim Mason-Adams, taught me how to have a loving family.

To my surprise, I also have an uncle who has taught me something as well. Jamie Mason taught me the skill that we all need to keep our lives balanced: how to have fun. I have tried to pass all of this down to my cousin—Fernando Young.

Lastly, I would like to thank the person who has given me all of herself. She has given me her love and understanding. She has also given me the best of everything to help make my life a success. She has also been the person whom I would like to model myself after. She is always there when I need someone to speak to. It is also just special to know that she is there. She is also there to help me with the emotional and mental skills that I have trouble with. Her name is Ms. Deborah Young.

I also thank God for being the person I can pray to. I thank Him for thinking of me and for doing what was necessary to take care of me.

# CHAPTER 16

## ACTIVITIES FOR HANDICAP CHILDREN

*C*hildren should not solely depend on family or friends for support, as this support system may be weak. It will not be there because families and friends usually do not know how to give what is considered to be good support.

But how can friends keep self-esteem and support going for these children, outside family member or friend of the family to help keep the family in line with the child. But most importantly, the child with the disorder needs to learn how to build up their own self-esteem. I admit that there are times when self-esteem will fail. You can feel low and down like everyone else around you. This is when you need to know how to uplift yourself.

Here, I have listed some activities that you and your family can do and participate in with your child. You have to know that your child has the same feelings that you do as a person. Their feelings also hurt like yours. Know that to understand your child's feelings, picture yours being a lot worse than you would normally express. Especially if your child can't express to you in words that you can understand.

There are other ways that you and your family can communicate with your child. You can draw pictures, write letters, play music and find a psychiatrist who could help you to understand your child's feelings. The effort you make in trying to understand your child will be effort that you will cherish for a long time in your life. Each conversation that you have with your child will then become very special. Also, have your other children learn how to socialize with your child. Then they, too, will have a special bond with their brother or sister that they can cherish. If you have to, share with your family any information necessary to help them in interacting with your child as well. Here is the list of possible activities for you and your child:

### Activities for Handicap Children

1) Telling family stories
2) Allowing the child to cook with you (messy or not)
3) Allowing the child to sew with you
4) Listening to your child.
5) Find a comfortable/possible activity for your child; these things can include music or art (painting, making objects).
6) Allow your child to help you; they will also learn from you as well.
7) Find a personal group that your child can attend.
8) Find a pet that your child can enjoy.
9) Teach the child anything/everything that you know.
10) Spend time in church with your child (most important).

Believe me, the feeling that your child will carry will be one that they will always carry. All of this will make the life with you and your child a very peaceful one. This is one feeling that, to this day, I will treasure in my heart. This feeling has also made those things possible because the way I felt about these achievements made it possible to have the desire to model and achieve goals for myself.

# CHAPTER 17

## TYPE OF RELATIONSHIP WITH YOUR CHILD

Your child, in their lifetime, will experience many different relationships. Some of those relationships may be good or bad. These relationships may look different on the outside, but in time, may give you the same type of feeling. Just not when you want it so it is important to take the time to teach your child the different types of emotions possible. Also, relate these emotions to different people. One type of expression that may come out of you, may come out differently in someone else. Your child may not get what they desire at one time in their life from a particular person, but may experience in later (easier for the other person) at a better time in life.

Here is a listing of the types of relationships possible and what they may look like:

Love: warm, affection, benevolence, charity, sexual passion, sweetheart

Examples: A person who gives gifts, talks to you constantly or occasionally, or is a helpful person.

There may be a person who can't express this love to your child not because they don't want to, but because they never learned how. If it does happen, it's when they feel comfortable.

Hate: dislike strongly: bear malice toward

Examples: A person who is a mean person, hollers a lot, difficult to understand or talk to.

This person may be this way not because they choose to be, but because it is the only way they know how to keep their pain away. They tend to be the person that you see less of. This is great because you won't become overwhelmed by their pain.

Strong: powerful; robust healthy; difficult to break

Weak: lacking strength; feeble; fragile; defenseless


"Strong" and Weak" are a team. They tend to work together. No one word is better than the other. You can get a positive or negative feeling from both. This depends on the situation and decision you make in dealing with the problem. So, these words can cause problems when they are related to you or to those around you. It may not be best to make the decision (right or wrong) based on the last one that was similar. You always have to come in with clean slate.

A strong person can become weak by expecting everything to be done for them, or by expecting everything to happen on its own. This is the person who sits back with their feet up. A weak person can become strong by doing the best to achieve and look like others around them. This is the person constantly moving and trying to do everything right.

These words can be used in many different ways. It depends on how you, as a person, chose to experience them. The choice is made by you. Just understand that your decision may have an effect on others; so just be careful.

# CHAPTER 18

## PHYSICAL, MENTAL, AND EMOTIONAL EXPERIENCES

These are experiences that I have had while living with my disorder. These experiences to me were very common with many of the medications that my doctors prescribed for me. The experiences that I am telling you about are called side effects. These side effects tend to affect one's brain, skin, eating habits, organs, and many of the things that we do naturally in our lives (like urination). Many other side effects are also possible. It is a very good idea to get pamphlets of information whenever you or your child are put on any new medication. This way, you will be familiar with the medication and will know how to live your life around the side effects.

There are possible side effects that will even help you to live a better life. One such side effect is the desire to eat a lot of vegetables and drink a lot of water and juices to help flush out your system. (This is because your stomach tightens.)

Possible side effects of this condition are:

1) Pain in the temporal lobe where mental and physical parts of the brain connect.
Example: can't say "Hello" and "Smile" at the same time.
2) Forced to live two separate lives---mental and physical
3) Physically weak all over
4) Live a nervous life---will bite nails or even hit stomach

5) A weak appetite that makes a person eat a lot of small meals, and food makes them feel tired; will have to eat lot of vegetables and drink a lot of liquids, but no hard sodas.

6) Can't exercise at all or play sports because of weak muscles

7) Hard time sleeping when sick

8) Hard time feeling emotionally good; will have to go to a psychiatrist; will also have to work hard in keeping up appearance.

9) Emotions match those of an old person

10) Sensitive to snow; it causes a person to stay out of it and only like it from the inside

11) Body is sensitive to cold weather; will have the desire to dress like an old person, having to wrap their whole body up.

12) Desire to like medication.

13) Have a memory problem that is so weak that one will have to write their emotions out because their memory is too weak to hold or get rid of them (by the person's choice) Example: Keeping happy emotions; discarding sad emotions. Remembering what is only spoken about often. Having to make a pattern to feel comfortable with who or what is going on around.

14) Problems in school with relating and learning.

15) Need to wear necklace or bracelet about condition.

16) Must learn to love themselves with condition.

17) Do best to think and live like a healthy person.

18) Constant sore throat that feels like tonsillitis.


Suggestions:

1) Parents pick one good friend that child can 'model' themselves after

2) Allow them to participate in an activity like music. Allow child to pick the instrument.

3) Activity may become child's career

4) Allow child to participate in programs to keep spirits up

# CHAPTER 19

## THE BIRTH OF A NEW FEELING—HAPPINESS

The word "Happy" is a very special word. This word has a feeling of being glad or lighthearted. When expressed, it's normally through the picture of a smile on a person's face. It's hard to believe that any person could live without this feeling. This feeling allows one to feel good about themselves. This feeling invites others into your life.

All of my life up to now, I've had to live without the expression of happiness. If I ever felt happy, the feeling only lasted for minutes at a time. This feeling, easy for others, was stressful for me—which also made the job of communicating difficult. Mental confusion would occur. So, my thoughts felt like what a messed-up screen looks like on a television. Now, for the first time, I am able to communicate with my feelings and an expression of being "happy."

The birth of this "happy" feeling feels like the birth of a child. Being able to own this feeling has made me feel like a new person. I can now learn how to live my life through this emotion first and not have to try to earn this feeling. This enjoyment of being happy never lasted very long.

This decision was made by the disorder and not by me. This emotion was stressful and tiring for my mind and body to carry. So, the experience of this feeling could only be experienced internally. When expressed, it was only done through the time spent conversing with others. Conversing with my epilepsy family kept the stress of finding this emotion from being difficult. I couldn't find this feeling, but my mind could without me "thinking" about being "happy" first.

## Poem #1

### Breaking the Chains

Breaking the Chains
Is hard to do
When there is nobody
There with you.

Some chains can be made soft
While other can be broken
Chains can be stiff like a token.

Chains need to bend
to make a chain bend
a chain needs to be softened.

As a chain softens
you will see some lights
with less fights.
As you become free
you feel like a tree
as your fights become less
you'll make yourself a beautiful chain
which is called a "Necklace."

Learning Statement: So, loosening or softening the chain means making yourself a stronger person to handle your own problems and not allowing them to build or to frighten you.

**Poem #2**

## Seeing & Can't Being

Sometimes I see
in other people
things that I want to be
that lurk
inside of me.
It's very hard
when I can't find
a very good way
to rest my mind.
I want to be
so many people
when people say:
"You can be, what you want to be
If you go on and try,"
I'm not going to say
that it's not true
but you also have to accept
that we can't always be
that person or group of people
that we want to be.


Learning Statement: So all you can do is accept who you are and what you can do. It's not your fault if you can't do what you truly want to do in your life because you're doing a lot more than most people—you're giving it your best shot!

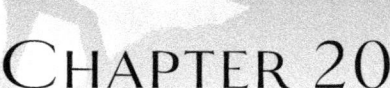

# CHAPTER 20

## GAMES

Families should have a family time together, whether through picnics, birthday parties, or just one-on-one. During these times, games should be played between children, adults, or both.

Board games are a lot of fun. They allow the child and even the adult a way to have fun while learning how to concentrate.

Puzzles are just as much fun. The enjoyment is the success of getting a puzzle piece in and finishing the puzzle itself.

My personal favorite is card games. Parties can be established around just one card game. Or better yet, card games can be a way of getting, teaching, and giving your child those skills that they need for school. I have listed several games below that are played by many people. (Or, just say, games that I've played myself.) As you go down the list, the games get harder and are intended more for adults (or just older, more developed minds).

### Child Game: FISH

1. Deal five cards, with a pile in the middle.
2. The following player (not the dealer) asks for a particular card from the player on the right. (Ex: "Do you have a King?")
3. The player gets a reply of "Yes" or "No."

4. If yes, the player receives the card and gets to ask again. If no, the player plucks from the deck. If the card matches any card in their hand, they can also lay it down.
5. The play goes to the next player to right.

## Child/Adult Game: CONCENTRATION

1. Shuffle and lay cards face down on the floor or table.

2. Pick two cards and turn over.

3. If the number or letters match, pick them up.

4. Continue if you have made a match.

5. If no match is made, then it's the next player's turn.

6. The player with the most matches win the game.

These two games will teach your child how to concentrate, learn their numbers, and develop a belief in winning.

## Child/Adult Game: "21" or BLACKJACK

Point System: A's = 1 or 11 points

K, Q, J's = 10 points

1 through 10 = the number on the cards

(ex. 6 = 6 points)

1. One card is dealt face down and another card is dealt fac up.

2. Player counts cards to come up to 21 points.

3. If score is low (ex: 10 points), a player may take a risk and ask for another card.

4. If score is high, like 18 points, a player may choose to stay the same.

5. The player with 21 points or the highest number without going over is 21 wins the game.

Older Person's Game: "500"

Point System: A, K, Q, J, 10's = 10 points

No.'s 1 through 9 = 5 points

1. Deal any odd number.

2. Turn one card over from the deck.

3. Matches are made in this format in order by the suit—spades, clubs, diamonds, or hearts.

4. Matches are also made by numbers or letters of different suits (ex: three or four sixes). You must have at least three cards to lay down or one or more to "Hit" with. "Hit" means to lay down cards that come in sequence with another player's matches.

5. Player picks a card from the deck or checks a card from the lay stack. If the player can use the card, he can lay the match out. (Note: If player picks from the lay stack of cards, he must be able to use that card at that particular time.)

6. After the player checks his hand for matches, and for matches from other players, he lays out a card on the stack allowing others to be able to see it.

7. The winner of the hand is the one who clears all cards from his hand.

8. Those with cards in their hand will subtract those points from their matches, else they will have to settle with a negative score for that hand.

9. The winner of the game is the one who scores "500" first.

## Older Person's Game: TONK

(Similar to 500)

1. Deal out 7 cards

2. Follow the count system in 500.

3. Don't pick up a starting card.

4. Pluck a card from deck and see as in 500 if it can be used.

5. If you believe you can use it, hold it or lay down a match with it.

6. You can also "Hit" your player as you do in 500.

7. Lay a card down. If there is a card that you believe you can use, pick it up and place it in your hand for later. Then lay another card on top of those cards that may also be exposed as well. (You can only check for the card that you "see," no cards below. So, it's like making a pile of face up cards.)

8. If you have one card in your hand, wait three rounds and lay the card down. Check all players' cards. Whoever has the least points in their hand wins that hand.

## Adult Game: SPADES

Two, three, or four players can play. If two players play, a third hand is dealt. If four players play, all cards except the two of spades and diamonds are taken out.

Game has three jokers:

a) Big joker, the one with a face on it.
b) Little joker, the plain looking joker.
c) Lastly, the two of spades.

Note: Write the words "Big" and "Little" on the cards if the jokers look too much alike.

1. Cards are dealt.

2. When played in teams (four people) the team agrees on a bid, else each person makes their own bid.

3. The bid is the number of suits they feel that they can achieve.

4. The player to the right of the dealer plays a card in their hand.

5. The other players try to beat the player in the same suit.

6. You play your cards according to the suit played.

7. The partner does his best not to beat out his partner; he can throw off with another low suit card like a club. If he has to, he can throw out (if he doesn't have a card in that particular suit) the spade (which is the cutting card), to win the book.

8. Whoever played the highest card or the spade, wins the book.

9. The person who wins the book, plays next.

10. This continues throughout the entire game.

11. If the player or the team does not make their bid, then a zero and the score becomes negative. If the player makes his bid and more, the score is positive. (Ex: 4 (bid), made 3, score is -40. (Ex: 4 (bid), made 4, score is +40). (Ex: 4 (bid), made 3 more, score is +43).

12. Player to the right deals next.

13. Game continues to the score of 500, which is the winner.